The Applying Knowledge from Nobody Is Coming to Save You Workbook

Learn from Scott Mann's book for Everyday Life

Manuel sagir

Disclaimer:

This workbook is an unofficial companion to the book *Nobody Is Coming to Save You: A Green Beret's Guide to Getting Big Sh*t Done**. It is intended to provide insights, analysis, and exercises related to the themes of the book. This workbook is not affiliated with or endorsed by the original author or publisher. All opinions, interpretations, and conclusions expressed in this workbook are those of the author, Manuel Sagir.

Table of content

Chapter 1: Understanding Rooftop Leadership: The Foundation of Action

Introduction to Rooftop Leadership

In today's fast-paced world, where chaos often reigns, the concept of leadership has evolved significantly. Traditional models of leadership often fail to address the complexities of modern environments characterized by uncertainty, low trust, and high stakes. This is where **Rooftop Leadership** comes into play, a transformative approach that emphasizes connection, understanding, and the ability to inspire action from a place of authenticity.

Rooftop Leadership is a term that encapsulates the idea of rising above the noise and chaos of everyday life to gain a broader perspective on challenges and opportunities. It encourages leaders to step back, observe, and then engage with those around them in a manner that fosters trust and collaboration. In this chapter, we will explore the foundational elements of Rooftop Leadership, its significance in various contexts, and how it can empower individuals to take meaningful action.

The Essence of Rooftop Leadership

At its core, Rooftop Leadership is about perspective and connection. Leaders who practice this approach understand that their role is not just to direct but to inspire. They see themselves as facilitators of change rather than mere authority figures. This mindset shift is crucial in creating an environment where individuals feel empowered to contribute, innovate, and take risks.

Key Elements of Rooftop Leadership

1. **Perspective Taking**: Rooftop leaders cultivate the ability to see situations from multiple angles. They recognize that every individual has a unique background and perspective, which influences their understanding of

events. By acknowledging these differences, leaders can create a more inclusive and empathetic environment.

2. **Building Trust**: Trust is the bedrock of effective leadership. Rooftop leaders prioritize building relationships based on honesty, transparency, and integrity. They understand that trust is not given but earned through consistent actions and open communication.

3. **Empowering Others**: A key aspect of Rooftop Leadership is the emphasis on empowering individuals within the team. Leaders who adopt this approach recognize that they do not have all the answers. Instead, they create spaces for team members to express their ideas, share their expertise, and take ownership of their work.

4. **Embracing Vulnerability**: Authentic leadership requires a willingness to be vulnerable. Rooftop leaders are not afraid to

admit their mistakes or uncertainties. This openness fosters a culture where others feel safe to do the same, leading to greater collaboration and innovation.

The Importance of Context in Leadership

Rooftop Leadership is particularly relevant in contexts where trust has eroded, and uncertainty prevails. Whether in corporate settings, community organizations, or even during times of crisis, leaders must navigate complex dynamics that require a nuanced understanding of human behavior.

The Corporate Landscape

In the corporate world, the effects of low trust and high stakes are evident. Employees may feel disengaged, communication may break down, and productivity may decline. Rooftop Leadership provides a framework for addressing these challenges by focusing on relationship-building and fostering a sense of belonging.

1. **Reconnecting with Employees**: In a corporate environment, leaders must take proactive steps to reconnect with their teams. This may involve regular check-ins, open forums for discussion, and recognizing individual contributions. By prioritizing connection, leaders can rebuild trust and create a more cohesive team.

2. **Navigating Change**: Organizations often face rapid changes that can lead to uncertainty among employees. Rooftop leaders can help navigate these transitions by providing clear communication, offering support, and encouraging feedback. This approach allows employees to feel involved and valued during times of change.

Community Leadership

In community organizations, Rooftop Leadership takes on a unique dimension. Leaders are often tasked with bringing diverse groups together to address common challenges. The principles of Rooftop Leadership can help facilitate collaboration and understanding among community members.

1. **Creating Inclusive Spaces**: Rooftop leaders understand the importance of creating spaces where all voices are heard. By actively seeking input from community members, leaders can ensure that decisions reflect the needs and perspectives of those they serve.

2. **Empowering Local Leaders**: Rooftop Leadership is not just about one individual leading the charge; it's about empowering others to step into leadership roles. By nurturing local leaders, Rooftop leaders can create a sustainable model for community engagement and activism.

The Power of Action in Rooftop Leadership

Rooftop Leadership is not just about theory; it is rooted in action. Leaders who embody this approach are motivated by a desire to make a difference. They take calculated risks, challenge the status quo, and inspire others to do the same.

1. **Leading by Example**: Rooftop leaders understand that their actions speak louder than words. By modeling the behaviors they wish to see in others, they create a culture of accountability and excellence. This includes demonstrating a commitment to continuous learning, ethical behavior, and a strong work ethic.

2. **Encouraging Initiative**: Rooftop leaders actively encourage team members to take initiative. They provide the support and resources necessary for individuals to pursue their ideas and projects. This not only fosters innovation but also instills a sense of ownership among team members.

Conclusion

In conclusion, Rooftop Leadership offers a powerful framework for navigating the complexities of modern leadership. By emphasizing perspective, trust, empowerment, and vulnerability, leaders can create environments where individuals feel valued and motivated to take action. As we move forward in this workbook, we will explore how to navigate low-trust environments, build authentic connections, overcome obstacles, and ultimately create lasting change. Rooftop Leadership is not just a theory; it is a practice that has the potential to transform lives, organizations, and communities.

Chapter 2: Navigating Low-Trust Environments: Strategies for Success

Understanding Low-Trust Environments

In our interconnected world, trust has become a precious commodity. Yet, low-trust environments—where skepticism, cynicism, and doubt flourish—are increasingly common. These settings can be found in various contexts, including workplaces, communities, and even global interactions. Understanding how to navigate such environments is crucial for effective leadership and meaningful engagement.

Low-trust environments often manifest as a result of broken promises, past failures, or systemic issues. In these contexts, individuals may feel isolated, disengaged, or fearful of taking risks. As a Rooftop Leader, it's essential to recognize the signs of low trust and implement strategies to foster a culture of collaboration, transparency, and connection.

The Impact of Low Trust on Leadership

Low trust can hinder productivity, stifle creativity, and foster toxic workplace cultures. When trust is lacking, team members may hesitate to share ideas, voice concerns, or collaborate effectively. This can lead to misunderstandings, conflicts, and a decline in morale.

Key Effects of Low Trust:

1. **Reduced Engagement:** Employees in low-trust environments are less likely to engage fully in their work. They may become apathetic, leading to decreased motivation and productivity.
2. **Increased Turnover:** A lack of trust can result in higher turnover rates as employees seek more supportive and transparent environments. This not only disrupts team dynamics but also incurs costs related to recruitment and training.

3. **Communication Breakdowns**: Communication often suffers in low-trust environments. Team members may withhold information, leading to misalignment and confusion about goals and expectations.

4. **Resistance to Change**: Individuals in low-trust settings may resist change initiatives, fearing that their concerns will not be heard or that they will be blamed for failures. This resistance can stall progress and innovation.

Strategies for Building Trust

As a Rooftop Leader, your role is to identify the underlying causes of low trust and implement strategies to rebuild it. Here are several actionable approaches to foster trust within your team or community:

1. Establish Open Communication

Open and honest communication is foundational to building trust. Create an environment where individuals feel safe to express their thoughts, concerns, and ideas. This can be achieved through regular check-ins, team meetings, and anonymous feedback channels.

- **Regular Updates**: Share updates on team goals, progress, and challenges. Transparency about decisions and processes fosters a sense of inclusion and trust.
- **Active Listening**: Practice active listening by giving your full attention to team members when they speak. Validate their feelings and perspectives, even if you don't agree with them.

2. Lead by Example

Demonstrate the behaviors you wish to see in your team. By modeling trustworthiness and accountability, you set the tone for others to follow. This includes admitting mistakes, taking responsibility, and being transparent about your decisions.

- **Be Vulnerable**: Sharing your own challenges and uncertainties can humanize you as a leader and encourage others to open up. This vulnerability helps to break down barriers and build trust.
- **Follow Through on Promises**: Consistently deliver on your commitments. If circumstances change, communicate openly about why and what steps you are taking to address the situation.

3. Foster Team Collaboration

Encourage collaboration among team members to build relationships and strengthen trust. When individuals work together towards common goals, they develop a sense of camaraderie and shared purpose.

- **Team-Building Activities**: Organize team-building exercises that promote collaboration and communication. These activities can help break down silos and foster stronger relationships.
- **Cross-Functional Projects**: Create opportunities for team members from different departments or backgrounds to collaborate on projects. This exposure to diverse perspectives can enhance understanding and trust.

4. Recognize and Celebrate Contributions

Acknowledge the contributions of team members regularly. Recognizing individual and team efforts fosters a positive environment where individuals feel valued and appreciated.

- **Public Recognition**: Celebrate achievements in team meetings or through company-wide communications.

Highlighting successes reinforces a culture of gratitude and recognition.

- **Personalized Feedback**: Offer personalized feedback that reflects an understanding of individual strengths and contributions. This demonstrates that you value each team member's unique role.

Navigating Conflicts in Low-Trust Environments

Conflicts are inevitable, especially in low-trust environments. However, how leaders approach and resolve conflicts can either exacerbate or alleviate tension.

Conflict Resolution Strategies

1. **Address Issues Early**: Don't allow conflicts to fester. Address issues as they arise to prevent escalation. Initiating open dialogues can help clarify misunderstandings and build trust.
2. **Facilitate Open Dialogue**: Create a safe space for individuals to express their

concerns. Encourage respectful discussions that focus on finding solutions rather than placing blame.

3. **Seek Common Ground**: Identify shared goals or interests among conflicting parties. Focusing on commonalities can help reduce tension and foster collaboration.

4. **Utilize Mediators if Necessary**: In more complex situations, consider involving neutral third parties to facilitate discussions. Mediators can help navigate difficult conversations and find equitable solutions.

Conclusion

Navigating low-trust environments is undoubtedly challenging, but it is not insurmountable. By employing the strategies outlined in this chapter, you can begin to foster an environment of trust and collaboration. As a Rooftop Leader, your commitment to transparency, active listening, and empowering others will create a culture where individuals feel valued and motivated to contribute.

As we move forward in this workbook, we will delve deeper into the importance of building authentic connections, overcoming obstacles, and creating lasting change. Remember, every step you take towards building trust is a step towards a more engaged, collaborative, and successful team.

Chapter 3: Building Authentic Connections: The Power of Human Interaction

The Importance of Human Connection

In a world increasingly dominated by technology and digital interactions, the value of authentic human connection cannot be overstated. While tools and platforms facilitate communication, they often lack the depth and emotional resonance that face-to-face interactions provide. Building authentic connections is not just a personal endeavor; it is a critical leadership skill that can transform teams, organizations, and communities.

Authentic connections are characterized by trust, empathy, and mutual respect. These connections foster a sense of belonging, encourage collaboration, and inspire individuals to work together toward shared goals. As Rooftop Leaders, understanding the power of these connections is essential for creating environments where people feel valued and empowered to contribute.

The Science of Connection

Research has shown that human connection is fundamental to our well-being. When we connect authentically with others, we experience a range of psychological and physiological benefits, including:

1. **Enhanced Well-Being**: Positive social interactions contribute to overall mental health and emotional resilience. Individuals who feel connected are less likely to experience feelings of loneliness and depression.

2. **Improved Performance**: Teams that prioritize authentic connections tend to perform better. When team members trust and understand one another, they are more likely to collaborate effectively and achieve common goals.

3. **Increased Engagement**: Employees who feel a sense of belonging and connection are more engaged in their work. This leads to higher job satisfaction and lower turnover rates.

4. **Stronger Resilience**: Authentic connections provide a support network during challenging times. Knowing that others have your back can help individuals navigate stress and adversity more effectively.

Strategies for Building Authentic Connections

Creating authentic connections requires intentional effort and commitment. Here are several strategies to help you cultivate meaningful relationships within your team or community:

1. Prioritize Active Listening

Active listening is a cornerstone of authentic communication. When you genuinely listen to others, you demonstrate that you value their perspectives and experiences. This fosters trust and encourages openness.

- **Eliminate Distractions**: When engaging in conversations, minimize distractions. Put away your phone, make eye contact, and focus entirely on the person speaking.
- **Reflect and Respond**: After listening, reflect on what was said and respond thoughtfully. This shows that you are not only hearing their words but also understanding their feelings and intentions.

2. Create Safe Spaces for Sharing

Establishing an environment where individuals feel safe to express themselves is crucial for building authentic connections. Safe spaces encourage vulnerability and open communication.

- **Encourage Openness**: Clearly communicate that all team members are welcome to share their thoughts and feelings without fear of judgment. Reinforce this by modeling openness in your own communication.

- **Facilitate Vulnerability**: Share your own experiences and challenges. By being vulnerable, you invite others to do the same, creating a culture of trust and authenticity.

3. Foster a Culture of Empathy

Empathy is the ability to understand and share the feelings of others. As a leader, cultivating empathy within your team can strengthen connections and promote collaboration.

- **Practice Perspective-Taking**: Encourage team members to consider situations from others' perspectives. This practice can foster understanding and reduce conflict.
- **Acknowledge Emotions**: Validate the emotions of others. Acknowledging their feelings shows that you care and helps create a supportive environment.

4. Celebrate Individuality

Each team member brings unique strengths, experiences, and perspectives to the table. Recognizing and celebrating these differences can strengthen connections and foster inclusivity.

- **Personalized Recognition**: Take time to acknowledge individual contributions and accomplishments. This recognition can be public or private, but it should reflect an understanding of each person's unique contributions.
- **Encourage Sharing**: Create opportunities for team members to share their personal stories, interests, and backgrounds. This fosters deeper connections and appreciation for one another.

Overcoming Barriers to Connection

While building authentic connections is essential, various barriers can hinder this process.

Recognizing and addressing these obstacles is vital for fostering meaningful relationships.

Common Barriers to Connection:

1. **Time Constraints:** In fast-paced environments, individuals may feel rushed and prioritize tasks over relationships. Make it a point to allocate time for connection-building activities.

2. **Fear of Vulnerability**: Many people fear showing their true selves due to concerns about judgment or rejection. As a leader, model vulnerability and create a safe space for others to express themselves.

3. **Cultural Differences**: Diverse teams may face challenges related to cultural misunderstandings. Promote cultural awareness and encourage open discussions about different perspectives.

4. **Digital Overload**: In an era of constant digital communication, individuals may feel

overwhelmed and disconnected. Encourage face-to-face interactions whenever possible and limit reliance on digital tools.

The Role of Connection in Leadership

As a Rooftop Leader, your ability to forge authentic connections will directly impact your effectiveness and the success of your team. Strong relationships create a foundation of trust that enables you to lead with influence and inspire others to take action.

Key Leadership Qualities Related to Connection:

1. **Authenticity**: Authentic leaders are true to themselves and their values. This authenticity fosters trust and encourages others to be open and honest.
2. **Empathy**: Empathetic leaders understand the needs and feelings of their team members. This understanding fosters strong

connections and creates a supportive work environment.

3. **Inclusivity**: Inclusive leaders value diversity and create opportunities for all voices to be heard. This fosters collaboration and strengthens team cohesion.

4. **Communication Skills**: Effective communicators build connections through clear, transparent, and empathetic communication. Strong communication skills are essential for fostering authentic relationships.

Conclusion

Building authentic connections is not just a nice-to-have; it is a necessity for effective leadership and team success. As you develop these connections, you will cultivate a culture of trust, collaboration, and engagement within your team.

In the next chapters, we will explore how to overcome obstacles, draw lessons from the field, and create lasting change. Remember that every connection you nurture contributes to a more resilient and empowered team.

Chapter 4: Overcoming Obstacles: Lessons from the Field

Introduction

In any leadership role, obstacles are an inevitable part of the journey. Understanding how to navigate and overcome these challenges is crucial for success. In this chapter, we will explore the common obstacles faced by leaders in low-trust environments and draw lessons from real-world experiences to help you develop strategies for overcoming these barriers.

Common Obstacles in Low-Trust Environments

1. **Communication Breakdowns**
   Effective communication is the backbone of any successful team. In low-trust environments, however, communication often falters. Misunderstandings, lack of clarity, and fear of backlash can create an

atmosphere where individuals hesitate to share their thoughts or concerns.

Lesson: Foster Open Channels

- **Establish Clear Communication Protocols**: Define how and when communication should occur within the team. Regular check-ins, open-door policies, and structured feedback sessions can help ensure that everyone feels heard.

- **Encourage Transparency**: Promote a culture where transparency is valued. When team members understand the rationale behind decisions, they are more likely to trust one another and feel comfortable sharing their perspectives.

2. **Resistance to Change**

Change is often met with resistance, especially in environments where individuals feel vulnerable. Fear of the unknown or concern about losing control can hinder progress and innovation.

Lesson: Involve Team Members in the Change Process

- **Engage Stakeholders Early**: When introducing changes, involve team members from the beginning. Soliciting input and addressing concerns can create buy-in and reduce resistance.

- **Communicate the Benefits**: Clearly articulate the advantages of the change. Highlight how it will improve workflows, enhance outcomes, and benefit team members personally.

3. **Lack of Trust**

Trust is the foundation of any successful relationship, and its absence can create significant obstacles. In low-trust environments, individuals may hesitate to collaborate, share information, or take risks.

Lesson: Build Trust Gradually

- ○ **Demonstrate Reliability**:
  Consistently deliver on promises and
  commitments. When team members
  see that you follow through on your
  word, trust will begin to develop.
- ○ **Encourage Small Wins**: Foster
  opportunities for collaboration on
  smaller projects. As team members
  experience success together, trust will
  grow, laying the groundwork for
  larger initiatives.

4. **Emotional Exhaustion**
   In high-stress environments, emotional
   exhaustion can take a toll on individuals and
   teams. When people feel overwhelmed, they
   may disengage or become resistant to
   collaboration.
   Lesson: Prioritize Well-Being

- ○ **Encourage Work-Life Balance**: Promote a culture that values self-care and work-life balance. Encourage team members to take breaks, recharge, and prioritize their mental health.
- ○ **Provide Support Resources**: Offer access to resources such as counseling services, workshops, or team-building activities that can help alleviate stress and foster resilience.

Lessons from the Field: Real-World Examples

Drawing on lessons from the field can provide invaluable insights into overcoming obstacles. Below are some real-world examples that illustrate effective strategies for addressing challenges in low-trust environments.

Case Study 1: A Nonprofit Organization Facing Communication Breakdowns

In a nonprofit organization focused on community development, leaders found that communication between departments was lacking. Team members often felt isolated and unaware of each other's projects. This disconnection led to duplicated efforts and frustration.

Solution: The leadership team implemented a weekly "Cross-Departmental Sync," where representatives from each department came together to share updates, challenges, and opportunities for collaboration. This initiative not only improved communication but also fostered a sense of camaraderie and teamwork across departments.

Case Study 2: A Corporate Team Resistant to Change

In a corporate setting, a team was hesitant to adopt a new project management software. Team members expressed concern about the learning curve and the potential for disruption to their workflows.

Solution: The team leader organized training sessions that emphasized the benefits of the new software. Additionally, they invited team members to be part of a pilot group, allowing them to provide feedback and address concerns early in the process. This hands-on approach facilitated a smoother transition and increased buy-in.

Case Study 3: A Military Unit Struggling with Trust

In a military unit, trust among team members was strained following a high-stress deployment. Team members were reluctant to share vulnerabilities, leading to misunderstandings and conflicts.

Solution: The commanding officer initiated a series of team-building exercises focused on vulnerability and open communication. By creating a safe environment where individuals could share their experiences and feelings, trust began to rebuild, improving team cohesion and performance.

Strategies for Overcoming Obstacles

Having explored various obstacles and real-world examples, it's essential to outline actionable strategies for overcoming challenges in low-trust environments:

1. **Conduct Regular Check-Ins**: Schedule regular one-on-one or team check-ins to assess team dynamics, address concerns, and encourage open dialogue.

2. **Create a Feedback Loop**: Implement a feedback mechanism where team members can share their thoughts anonymously. This can provide insights into issues that may be affecting trust and collaboration.

3. **Celebrate Progress**: Acknowledge and celebrate individual and team accomplishments, no matter how small. This practice fosters a positive atmosphere and reinforces a sense of shared purpose.

4. **Invest in Team Development**: Prioritize training and development opportunities that enhance team skills and strengthen

relationships. Workshops on communication, conflict resolution, and emotional intelligence can be invaluable.

5. **Encourage Peer Support**: Foster a culture where team members support one another. This can involve mentorship programs, buddy systems, or informal check-ins to ensure everyone feels connected and valued.

Conclusion

Overcoming obstacles in low-trust environments is a challenge, but it is not insurmountable. By implementing effective strategies, drawing on real-world lessons, and fostering a culture of authenticity and connection, leaders can navigate these challenges with confidence.

In the next chapter, we will explore the transformative power of creating lasting change and how to implement sustainable solutions in your organization or community. Remember that every obstacle you face is an opportunity for growth, both for yourself and your team.

Chapter 5: Creating Lasting Change: A Path Forward

Introduction

Creating lasting change in any organization or community requires commitment, vision, and a well-structured approach. In low-trust environments, the challenge is even greater. This chapter will explore the essential steps to facilitate meaningful and sustainable change, drawing on practical strategies and real-world examples. By understanding the dynamics of change and the importance of a collective vision, leaders can cultivate an environment where transformation thrives.

Understanding Change Dynamics

1. **The Change Curve**
   The change curve illustrates the emotional journey individuals undergo when faced

with change. This curve typically includes several stages: denial, anger, bargaining, depression, and acceptance. Understanding these stages can help leaders anticipate reactions and provide appropriate support. **Lesson**: Recognize and Address Emotions

- **Acknowledge Feelings**: When introducing change, validate the feelings of team members. Allowing them to express their concerns can create a sense of safety and facilitate the transition.
- **Provide Support During Transitions**: Offer resources such as counseling, workshops, or peer support groups to help individuals navigate their emotions throughout the change process.

2. **Creating a Compelling Vision**
A clear and inspiring vision is essential for guiding change efforts. When individuals

understand the "why" behind the change, they are more likely to engage and commit to the process.

Lesson: Craft a Shared Vision

- **Involve Team Members in Vision Creation**: Solicit input from team members to ensure that the vision reflects collective aspirations. This inclusivity fosters ownership and investment in the change process.

- **Communicate the Vision Effectively**: Use various communication channels to share the vision consistently. Visual aids, storytelling, and frequent updates can reinforce the message and maintain enthusiasm.

3. **Establishing Clear Goals and Metrics**
Setting clear, achievable goals is crucial for measuring progress and maintaining momentum. Establishing metrics allows

leaders to track the effectiveness of change initiatives and make necessary adjustments.

Lesson: Set SMART Goals

- ○ **Specific, Measurable, Achievable, Relevant, Time-bound**: Ensure that goals meet these criteria to provide clarity and direction. For example, instead of setting a vague goal like "improve team communication," set a SMART goal such as "increase weekly team check-ins to three times per week by the end of the quarter."
- ○ **Celebrate Milestones**: Acknowledge achievements along the way, reinforcing motivation and commitment to the overall vision.

Strategies for Creating Lasting Change

1. **Foster a Culture of Continuous Improvement**

   A culture of continuous improvement

encourages team members to seek opportunities for growth and innovation. This mindset is vital for sustaining change efforts.

- **Encourage Experimentation**: Allow team members to test new ideas without fear of failure. Emphasize that mistakes are part of the learning process and should be viewed as opportunities for growth.
- **Implement Regular Feedback Loops**: Create systems for ongoing feedback to assess progress, identify areas for improvement, and celebrate successes.

2. **Empower Leaders at All Levels**

Change should not be solely driven from the top down; it requires the involvement of leaders at all levels of the organization. Empowering individuals to take ownership of the change process can enhance commitment and accountability.

- ○ **Identify Change Champions**: Recognize and support individuals within the organization who demonstrate enthusiasm and commitment to the change initiative. Equip them with the tools and resources needed to inspire others.
- ○ **Encourage Decision-Making at All Levels**: Allow team members to make decisions related to their roles. This empowerment fosters a sense of ownership and accountability.

3. **Leverage Technology for Communication and Collaboration**

In today's digital age, technology plays a vital role in facilitating communication and collaboration. Utilizing the right tools can enhance transparency and streamline processes.

- **Adopt Collaboration Tools**: Implement tools that facilitate real-time collaboration and communication, such as project management software, video conferencing platforms, and shared document repositories.
- **Utilize Data Analytics**: Leverage data to track progress, identify trends, and make informed decisions. Data-driven insights can guide the change process and demonstrate its impact.

4. **Build Partnerships and Alliances**

Collaborating with external organizations, stakeholders, or community groups can amplify change efforts. Building partnerships enhances resources, expertise, and support.

- **Identify Synergistic Partners**: Seek out organizations or individuals whose goals align with your change

initiative. Collaborating can lead to
shared resources, knowledge, and
increased impact.

- ○ **Engage Stakeholders Early**: Involve
  key stakeholders in the planning and
  implementation phases of change
  initiatives. Their input can provide
  valuable perspectives and increase
  buy-in.

Real-World Examples of Lasting Change

Examining successful examples of lasting change
can provide inspiration and practical insights. Here
are three notable cases:

Case Study 1: A School District's Curriculum Overhaul

In a struggling school district, leaders recognized
the need for a comprehensive curriculum overhaul
to improve student outcomes. The change was met
with resistance from teachers and parents, who
feared disruption.

Solution: The district engaged teachers, parents, and community members in a collaborative process to redefine the curriculum. Through workshops and focus groups, they gathered input, addressed concerns, and developed a shared vision for the future. This inclusive approach led to successful implementation and improved student performance.

Case Study 2: A Corporation's Diversity and Inclusion Initiative

A large corporation aimed to enhance its diversity and inclusion efforts in response to increasing societal demands for equity. Initial efforts were met with skepticism from employees who felt the initiative lacked authenticity.

Solution: The leadership team established a Diversity and Inclusion Task Force comprising employees from various levels and backgrounds. The task force developed a clear vision, set measurable goals, and regularly communicated progress to the entire organization. By empowering employees to lead the initiative, the corporation fostered a culture of inclusion and accountability.

Case Study 3: A Community's Environmental Sustainability Efforts

In a community facing environmental challenges, residents rallied to create a sustainable future. Initial attempts at change faced resistance from those who felt the effort would be too costly and disruptive.

Solution: Community leaders organized town hall meetings to engage residents in discussions about sustainability. By addressing concerns, sharing success stories from similar communities, and highlighting the long-term benefits, the initiative gained traction. Over time, the community implemented various sustainable practices, leading to a cleaner and healthier environment.

Conclusion

Creating lasting change is an intricate process that requires dedication, vision, and the collaboration of all stakeholders. By understanding change dynamics, fostering a culture of continuous improvement, empowering leaders at all levels, leveraging technology, and building partnerships, organizations can navigate the complexities of transformation.

In the end, lasting change is not just about achieving specific goals; it's about creating a mindset that embraces growth, connection, and resilience. As you embark on your journey to create lasting change, remember that every step forward is an opportunity for progress, connection, and transformation.

The journey ahead may be challenging, but with the right strategies and a commitment to action, you can navigate the path forward and inspire others to join you in creating a better future.

_____

_____

_____

_____

_____

_____

Made in United States
Troutdale, OR
01/04/2025

Made in United States
Troutdale, OR
01/04/2025

27614194R00037